2011

Happy Birthday

FAY

your
s...

.... Reason t...

D0938002

101 reasons
i love
GOD

Paul & Caroline Brownlow

101 Reasons I Love God

© 2009 Brownlow Gifts
6309 Airport Freeway, Fort Worth, Texas 76117

Scripture quotations are taken from the following versions:

ISBN-13: 978-159177-541-6

Printed in Singapore

101 reasons
i love
GOD

Written and Compiled by
Paul and Caroline Brownlow

i love
God because

He loved me first. He took the initiative.

He was willing to risk rejection, and let

me choose to love Him or not.

. . . .

We love him, because he first loved us.
1 John 4:19 (KJV)

i love
God because

He is always strong and ready to

help me when I am in trouble.

. . . .

God is our refuge and strength, a very present help in trouble.
Psalm 46:1 (NKJV)

i love **God** because

He has prepared a place in heaven that is beyond description where I will live with Him forever. My room is already reserved! I can't even imagine how wonderful it will be.

. . . .

In my Father's house are many rooms; I am going there to prepare a place for you. No eye has seen, no ear has heard, no mind has conceived what God has prepared for those who love him.
John 14:2,3; 1 Corinthians 2:9 (NIV)

i love
God because

He knows what I am really like and

still loves me. But He loves me too

much to let me stay this way.

. . . .

For he knows how we are formed, he remembers
that we are dust. Psalm 103:14 (NIV)

i love
God because

His angels constantly surround

me and protect me.

. . . .

The angel of the Lord encamps around those who fear him,
and he delivers them. For he will command his angels to
guard you in all your ways. Psalm 34:7; 91:11 (NIV)

i love
God because

He wants me to be confident in His love —

to know for sure He is going to help me

when I come to Him. He doesn't want

me to be timid or insecure.

. . . .

Let us then approach the throne of grace with confidence, so that we may receive mercy and find grace to help us in our time of need. Hebrews 4:16 (NIV)

i love God because

He doesn't judge by outward appearances,

like I do, but He looks at my heart.

. . . .

For the Lord does not see as man sees; for man looks at the
outward appearance, but the Lord looks at the heart.
1 Samuel 16:7 (NKJV)

i love
God because

He doesn't make me love Him.

He could force me to love Him, but

He doesn't. He is respectful and

asks to be invited into my heart.

. . . .

*Look! Here I stand at the door and knock. If you hear me
calling and open the door, I will come in, and we will share a
meal as friends. Revelation 3:20 (NLT)*

i love
God because

He doesn't want me to live in **fear.**

More than anything else, **Jesus** told His

disciples, **"Don't be afraid!"**

You of little faith, why are you so afraid? Do not be afraid.
Don't be afraid. Matthew 8:26; 10:28,31 (NIV)

i love **God** because

He gave me His **Word** so that

I could **know** Him and be

ready to **work** with Him.

*All Scripture is inspired by God and is profitable for
teaching, for rebuking, for correcting, for training in
righteousness, so that the man of God may be
complete, equipped for every good work.*
2 Timothy 3:16,17 (CSB)

i love **God** because

when I sin, He does not give me

the "silent treatment" or

the "cold shoulder" for awhile.

He is always quick to forgive.

. . . .

But you, O Lord, are a compassionate and gracious God,
slow to anger, abounding in love and faithfulness.
Psalm 86:15 (NIV)

i love
God because

He will not give up on me, even if others

do. He keeps on until He finishes His work

in me. He's not done with me yet.

. . . .

I am sure of this, that He who started a good work in you will carry it on to completion until the day of Christ Jesus.
Philippians 1:6 (CSB)

i love
God because

He never allows me to be tempted

or suffer more than I can stand.

He knows my limits.

. . . .

No temptation has seized you except what is common to man.
And God is faithful; he will not let you be tempted beyond
what you can bear. But when you are tempted, he will also
provide a way out so that you can stand up under it.
1 Corinthians 10:13 (NIV)

i love
God because

He is my loving shepherd

and takes care of me.

I really need a shepherd.

. . . .

The Lord is my shepherd; I shall not want.
Psalm 23 (KJV)

i love God because

when I am upset and troubled, He gently

comforts me with a tender love.

. . . .

The Lord your God is with you; he is mighty to save. He will take great delight in you; he will quiet you with his love, he will rejoice over you with singing.
Zephaniah 3:17 (NIV)

i love **God** because

He doesn't discriminate or play favorites

with His children. He loves us all, even

me, equally. No one is second-class.

. . . .

For as many of you as have been baptized into Christ have put on Christ. There is no Jew or Greek, slave or free, male or female; for you are all one in Christ Jesus.
Galatians 3:27,28 (CSB)

i love **God** because

He is the greatest – there is no one like

Him in the universe. No one else can do

the things He can do. No one.

. . . .

There is none like you among the gods, O Lord, nor are there any works like yours. For you are great and do wondrous things; you alone are God. Psalm 86:8, 10 (ESV)

i love
God because

He wants everybody to be

saved and go to heaven, not

just a few special people.

. . . .

The Lord is not slow in keeping his promise. He is patient with
you, not wanting anyone to perish, but wanting everyone to come to
repentance. God our Savior ... wants all men to be saved.
2 Peter 3:9; 1 Timothy 2:3,4 (NIV)

i love **God** because

He comes **near** to me when I want to be **close** to Him. Of course, **He** wants to be close **all the time.**

So give yourselves humbly to God. Resist the devil and he will flee from you. And when you draw close to God, God will draw close to you.
James 4:7,8 (NLT)

i love
God because

He **carries** me in His arms,

like a **lamb**, close to

His **heart.**

He tends his flock like a shepherd: He gathers the
lambs in his arms and carries them close to his heart;
He gently leads those that have young.
Isaiah 40:11 (NIV)

i love
God because

He always keeps His promises –

all of them. I break promises, or

forget I even made them.

But He never does.

. . . .

*You know with all your heart and soul that not one
of all the good promises the Lord your God gave you
has failed. Every promise has been fulfilled; not one
has failed. Joshua 23:14 (NIV)*

i love **God** because

He lets me be His friend.

. . . .

You are My friends, if you do what I command you.
John 15:14 (NASB)

i love **God** because

He listens to Jesus talking to Him on my behalf.

. . . .

Christ Jesus, who died – more than that, who was raised to
life – is at the right hand of God and is interceding for us.
Romans 8:34 (NIV)

i love
God because

He gives me second chances over

and over to obey and serve Him.

. . . .

But when he came to himself, he said, "How many of my father's hired servants have more than enough bread, but I perish here with hunger! I will go to my father and say I have sinned." But while he was still a long way off, his father saw him and felt compassion, and ran and embraced him and kissed him.
Luke 15:17-20 (ESV)

i love **God** because

He is tenderhearted. He and His

angels rejoice when I repent.

. . . .

"Rejoice with me, for I have found the coin which I had lost!" In the same way, there is joy in the presence of the angels of God over one sinner who repents.
Luke 15:9,10 (NASB)

i love God because

when He sees trouble and grief,

He does something about it. He is

a God of action, not just talk.

. . . .

But you, O God, do see trouble and grief;
you consider it to take it in hand.
Psalm 10:14 (NIV)

i love
God because

He gives me His tender mercies fresh

every morning. His grace never runs out

or runs dry; it is always there.

. . . .

The steadfast love of the Lord never ceases; his mercies never come to an end; they are new every morning; great is your faithfulness. Lamentations 3:22,23 (ESV)

i love God because

He can do greater things with me and

through me than I have ever even

thought of. He can use even me!

· ·

Now to Him who is able to do above and beyond all that we ask or think – according to the power that works in you – to Him be glory in the church and in Christ Jesus.
Ephesians 3:20,21 (CSB)

i love God because

He has saved all my tears in a

bottle. He knows every time

I have cried. He cares.

. . . .

You have seen me tossing and turning through the night.
You have collected all my tears and preserved them in
your bottle! You have recorded every one in your book.
Psalm 56:8 (NLT)

i love
God because

He has **shown** me how to get

through suffering. I have a **guide** to

lead me through.

·ⓢ·ⓢ·ⓢ·ⓢ·ⓢ·ⓢ·ⓢ·ⓢ·ⓢ·

For to this you were called, because Christ also suffered for us,
leaving us an example, that you should follow His steps.
1 Peter 2:21 (NKJV)

i love **God** because

He can **make up** for the

wasted years in my life.

Don't we **all** have some of those?

⊙·⊙·⊙·⊙·⊙·⊙·⊙·⊙·⊙·

*I will repay you for the years that
the swarming locust ate.*
Joel 2:25 (CSB)

i love God because

He always tells me the truth.

He cannot lie to me or anyone;

God is not a liar.

. . . .

He has given us both his promise and his oath, two things we can completely count on, for it is impossible for God to tell a lie. Hebrews 6:18 (NLT)

i love
God because

He gives me the ability to produce wealth

and resources. None of it is my own genius

– it is all from God.

. . . .

He fed you with manna in the wilderness so that you would become humble and your trust in him would grow. He did it so that you would never feel that it was your own power and might that made you wealthy. Always remember that it is the Lord your God who gives you power to become rich.
Deuteronomy 8:16-18 (NLT)

i love **God** because

He comes close to me when

I am brokenhearted.

. . . .

The Lord is near the brokenhearted; He saves those crushed in spirit. Psalm 34:18 (CSB)

i love **God** because

He thinks about me all the time.

. . . .

O Lord, what is man that you care for him, that you think of him? You made him a little lower than the angels and crowned him with glory and honor. Psalm 144:3; 8:5 (NIV)

i love **God** because

even in my old age, He can make me

enthusiastic and productive. I can be

full of life, not just breathing,

all the way to the end.

. . . .

*Planted in the house of the Lord, they will still
bear fruit in old age, healthy and green.
Psalm 92:13, 14 (CSB)*

i love **God** because

He has given me His Holy Spirit to live

within me to empower me, and as a

down payment for heaven.

. . . .

*In him you also, when you heard the word of truth, the gospel
of your salvation, and believed in him, were sealed with the
promised Holy Spirit, who is the guarantee of our inheritance
until we acquire possession of it. God's spirit dwells in you.*
Ephesians 1:13,14; 1 Corinthians 3:16 (ESV)

i love
God because

He never gets tired or worn out. When

I get tired, He makes me strong again.

He renews my strength daily.

. . . .

He will not grow tired or weary, and his understanding no one can fathom. He gives strength to the weary and increases the power of the weak. Even youths grow tired and weary, and stumble and fall; but those who hope in the Lord will renew their strength. They will soar on wings like eagles; they will run and not grow weary, they will walk and not be faint.
Isaiah 40:28-31 (NIV)

i love **God** because

He knows what I will need and provides

for it ahead of time. He is the Great Provider,

always there for me.

· ·

Isaac spoke up and said, "The fire and wood are here, but where is the lamb for the offering?" Abraham answered, "God himself will provide the lamb my son." And the two of them went on together.... So Abraham called that place The Lord Will Provide.
Genesis 22:7-14 (NIV)

i love God because

Jesus paid for my sins, all of them, and

declared the bill "paid". My debt has

already been paid!

. . . .

Knowing that all things had already been accomplished, Jesus said,
"It is finished." And he bowed His head and gave up His spirit.
John 19:28-30 (NASB)

i love God because

He **cares for** the land He created.

He waters it so I can have **food** and

drink and **nourishment.**

You care for the land and water it; you enrich it abundantly.
The streams of God are filled with water to provide the
people with grain. Psalm 65:9 (NIV)

i love
God because

He will **never** leave me or run out on

me. I can **always** count on **Him.**

God has said, "Never will I leave you; never will I forsake you." So we say with confidence, "The Lord is my helper; I will not be afraid. What can people do to me?"
Hebrews 13:5,6 (NIV)

i love
God because

He gives me everything I want – when I

find my greatest joy and delight in Him. I

want to want what He wants.

. . . .

*Take delight in the Lord, and He will give you your
heart's desires. Psalm 37:4 (CSB)*

i love **God** because

He has called me by my name

to be His child. He knows my name!

I belong to Him!

. . . .

Don't be afraid, for I have ransomed you. I have called you by name; you are mine. Isaiah 43:1 (NLT)

i love **God** because

He gives me courage for tough times

and the strength I need.

. . . .

When I called, you answered me; you made me bold and stouthearted. Psalm 138:3 (NIV)

i love **God** because

His presence in my life gives me great joy.

. . . .

Splendor and majesty you bestow on him. For you make him most blessed forever; you make him glad with the joy of your presence. Psalm 21:5,6 (ESV)

i love **God** because

He knew I couldn't keep all the rules,

or be good enough to save myself.

I needed grace!

. . . .

But because of his great love for us, God, who is rich in mercy, made us alive with Christ even when we were dead in our transgressions – it is by grace you have been saved.
Ephesians 2:4,5 (NIV)

i love **God** because

He has given me everything I really need

to be His child here on earth and forever.

. . . .

His divine power has given us everything we need for life and godliness through our knowledge of him who called us by his own glory and goodness. Through these he has given us his very great and precious promises, so that through them you may participate in the divine nature and escape the corruption in the world.
2 Peter 1:3,4 (NIV)

i love God because

He can perform miracles. But even

when He chooses not to intervene,

I still trust Him.

. . . .

You are the God of miracles and wonders! You still demonstrate Your awesome power. Psalm 77:14 (NLT)

i love **God** because

He will not let anything pull me

away from Him and His love.

. . . .

In all these things we are more than victorious through Him who loved us. For I am persuaded that neither death nor life, nor angels, nor rulers, nor things present, not things to come, nor powers, nor height, nor depth, nor any other created thing will have the power to separate us from the love of God that is in Christ Jesus our Lord!
Romans 8:37-39 (CSB)

i love God because

He is making my spiritual body stronger

every day, even though my physical

body is getting weaker and falling apart.

. . . .

Therefore we do not lose heart. Even though our outward man is perishing, yet the inward man is being renewed day by day.
2 Corinthians 4:16 (NIV)

i love **God** because

I can turn to **Him** when I am in trouble.

He is **the One** I go to. Of course,

He also likes for **me** to come

to Him when I'm **not** in trouble.

I love You, Lord, my strength. The Lord is my rock, my fortress and my deliverer, my God, my mountain where I seek refuge, my shield and the horn of my salvation, my stronghold. I called to the Lord, who is worthy of praise, and I was saved from my enemies.
Psalm 18:1-3 (CSB)

i love **God** because

He is **always** good to me, and

wants only **good** things for me.

He is not trying to **hurt** me or

catch me doing something wrong.

For the Lord is always good. He is always loving and kind, and his faithfulness goes on and on to each succeeding generation. No good thing will he withheld from those who walk along his paths.
Psalm 100:5; 84:11 (NLT)

i love **God** because

He is not moody or undependable.

He doesn't change the rules on me.

He is the same every day.

. . . .

Jesus Christ is the same yesterday and today
and forever. I am the Lord, I do not change.
Hebrews 13:8; Malachi 3:6 (NKJV)

i love **God** because

He hears me when I cry.

· ·

The Lord has heard my weeping, the Lord has heard my cry for mercy; the Lord accepts my prayer. Psalm 6:8,9 (NIV)

i love **God** because

He gave the most precious gift He had for me.

· ·

For God loved the world in this way: He gave His one and only son, so that everyone who believes in Him will not perish but have eternal life. John 3:16 (CSB)

i love
God because

He cares about the oppressed and needy,

the downtrodden and weak. He loves us

all, not just the rich and powerful.

. . . .

I will arise and defend the oppressed, the poor, the needy.
I will rescue them as they have longed for me to do. The Lord's
promise is sure. Psalm 12:5,6 (NLT)

i love
God because

He gets up when He hears me call. Like a

mother "gets up" when she hears her child

call or cry, God gets up and comes to me.

. . . .

The Lord longs to be gracious to you; he rises to show
you compassion. Blessed are all who wait for him.
Isaiah 30:18 (NIV)

i love
God because

He takes my meager, little efforts and

multiplies them to accomplish big things.

I just have to offer them to Him to use.

. . . .

"We have here only five loaves of bread and two fish," they answered. "Bring them here to me," he said. Then he gave them to the disciples and to the people. They all ate and were satisfied. Matthew 14:17-21 (NIV)

i love **God** because

He goes before me and makes

the road easier. He smoothes

out the rough spots.

. . . .

Trust in the Lord with all your heart, and do not lean upon your own understanding. In all your ways acknowledge him, and he will make straight your paths. Proverbs 3:5,6 (ESV)

i love God because

He has unlimited and unbelieveable

patience with me.

. . . .

But God had mercy on me so that Christ Jesus could use me as an example to show everyone how patient he is with even the worst sinners, so that others will realize that they, too, can have everlasting life. 1 Timothy 1:16 (NLT)

i love **God** because

His unfailing love is "priceless."

No amount of money can buy it.

. . . .

*How priceless is your unfailing love! Both high and low
among men find refuge in the shadow of your wings.
Psalm 36:7 (NIV)*

i love **God** because

He will always **protect**

me simply because I **love** Him. And

He **knows** who loves Him.

"Because he loves me," says the Lord, "I will rescue him;
I will protect him, for he acknowledges my name. He will
call upon me, and I will answer him."
Psalm 91:14,15 (NIV)

i love **God** because

He is the Supreme Eternal God of

the Universe, not a benevolent

grandfather who can be manipulated.

I want a God who is really God.

God, the blessed and only Ruler, the King of kings and Lord of lords, who alone is immortal and who lives in unapproachable light, whom no one has seen or can see. To him be honor and might forever. 1 Timothy 6:15,16 (NIV)

i love **God** because

He rescues me from my enemies.

Most of my enemies don't look

violent; they come offering pleasure

or contentment or gratification.

. . . .

He reached down from on high and took hold of me; He pulled me out of deep waters. He rescued me from my powerful enemy and from those who hated me, for they were too strong for me, but the Lord was my support. He rescued me because He delighted in me.
Psalm 18:16-19 (CSB)

i love
God because

He wants a relationship with me. He

wants me to pray in order to get close to

Him, not just to get things from Him.

· ·

*Your father knows what you need before
you ask him. Pray then like this....*
Matthew 6:8-13 (ESV)

i love God because

He doesn't play "Hide and Seek"

with me. He is not hard to find. I just

have to genuinely want to find Him.

. . . .

You will seek me and find me, when you seek me
with all your heart. I will be found by you.
Jeremiah 29:13,14 (ESV)

i love
God because

He always watches over me. I am

not all alone or on my own.

. . . .

*For the Lord watches over all the plans and
paths of godly men. Psalm 1:6 (TLB)*

i love
God because

He is perfect in every way. He is

the only perfect one.

. . . .

*What a God He is! How perfect in every way! All His
promises prove true. Psalm 18:30 (NLT)*

i love God because

He gives me the energy to accomplish

His purpose for me. I don't have to depend

solely on my own human resources.

. . . .

So everywhere we go we talk about Christ to all who will listen, teaching them as well as we know how. We want to present each one to God, perfect because of what Christ has done for each of them. This is my work, and I can do it only because Christ's mighty energy is at work within me.
Colossians 1: 28, 29 (NLT)

i love
God because

He knows when I make even the

smallest effort to reach out to Him.

He waits to be wanted.

. . . .

"If I only touch His cloak, I will be healed." Jesus turned and saw her. "Take heart, daughter, your faith has healed you." Matthew 9:21,22 (NIV)

i love
God because

He carries my problems every day.

Who else will do that?

. . . .

Praise be to the Lord, to God our Savior, who daily bears our burdens. Psalm 68:19 (NIV)

i love
God because

He listens to me when I call. The

God of the universe listens to me!

· ·

I love the Lord, for he heard my voice; he heard my cry for mercy. Because he turned his ear to me, I will call on him as long as I live. Psalm 116:1,2 (NIV)

i love **God** because

He **guarantees** me I will **live**

eternally with **Him** after death here.

For the trumpet will sound, the dead will be raised imperishable, and we will be changed. The sting of death is sin, and the power of sin is the law. But thanks be to God! He gives us the victory through our Lord Jesus Christ. 1 Corinthians 15:52-57 (NIV)

i love God because

He has taken **care** of me since I was **born**, and will **continue** to care for me as **long** as I **live**.

I created you and cared for you since you were born. I will be your God through all your lifetime, yes, even when your hair is white with age. Isaiah 46:3 (NLT)

i love **God** because

He lets me help Him, to be a

co-worker in His plan to save

the world. I am not a nobody.

. . . .

For we are God's fellow workers.
1 Corinthians 3:9 (ESV)

i love God because

He loves me too much not to correct

me. He does what is best for me.

Of course I had to become a parent

to really understand this.

. . . .

Our earthly fathers trained us for a few brief years, doing the best for us that they knew how, but God's correction is always right and for our best good, that we may share in his holiness. Being punished isn't enjoyable while it is happening – it hurts! But afterwards we can see the results a quiet growth in grace and character. Hebrews 12:10,11 (NLT)

i love **God** because

He suffers when I suffer.

· ·

The Lord said, "I have indeed seen the misery of my people in Egypt. I have heard them crying out, and I am concerned about their suffering. So I have come down to rescue them."
Exodus 3:7,8 (NIV)

i love **God** because

He has given me a divine "makeover."

· ·

How differently I feel now! When someone becomes a Christian he becomes a brand new person inside. He is not the same anymore. A new life has begun!
2 Corinthians 5:16,17 (NLT)

i love
God because

He is the God of surprises. He is not

hemmed in or controlled by difficult or

impossible circumstances like I am.

. . . .

Moses answered the people, "Do not be afraid. Stand firm and you will see the deliverance the Lord will bring you today. The Egyptians you see today you will never see again. The Lord will fight for you; you need only be still." Then the Lord said to Moses, "Raise your staff and stretch out your hand over the sea to divide the water so that the Israelites can go through the sea on dry ground." Exodus 14:13-16 (NIV)

i love **God** because

He is generous. He wants to open the

"windows of heaven" and pour out more

blessings on me than I can imagine.

. . . .

Bring all the tithes into the storehouse; if you do, I will open up the windows of heaven for you and pour out a blessing so great you won't have room enough to take it in! Try it! Let me prove it to you! Malachi 3:10 (NLT)

i love **God** because

He reaches out to people who

have been rejected. He doesn't

mind getting His hands dirty.

. . . .

Jesus stretched out his hand and touched him.
Immediately his leprosy was cleansed!
Matthew 8:3 (ESV)

i love **God** because

He has given me the weapons to

defend myself and promised to protect

me against Satan. We need weapons;

we all live in "Lion Country."

. . . .

Be strong in the Lord and in his mighty power. Put on the full armor of God so that you can take your stand against the devil's schemes. Your enemy, the devil, prowls around like a roaring lion looking for someone to devour. But the Lord is faithful, and he will strengthen and protect you from the evil one.
Ephesians 6:10,11; 1 Peter 5:8; 2 Thessalonians 3:3 (NIV)

i love **God** because

He forgives me and forgets all

about my sins. I don't understand this,

but I am extremely grateful for it.

. . . .

*For I will forgive their wrongdoing and never again
remember their sin. Jeremiah 31:34 (CSB)*

i love **God** because

He will always take care of me

even if my family forsakes me.

Even if my father and mother abandon me,
the Lord cares for me. Psalm 27:10 (CSB)

i love
God because

His Spirit helps me when

I don't know how to pray.

In the same way the Spirit also joins to help in our weakness, because we do not know what to pray for as we should, but the Spirit Himself intercedes for us. Romans 8:26 (CSB)

i love **God** because

He cares so much for me.

I am precious to Him!

. . . .

Humble yourselves therefore under the mighty hand of God, so that He may exalt you in due time, casting all your cares upon Him, because He cares for you. 1 Peter 5:6,7 (CSB)

i love **God** because

no matter how bad things get

here on earth, He is still in control.

I need to remember that.

. . . .

Woe to him who piles up stolen goods. Woe to him who builds his realm by unjust gain. Woe to him who builds a city with bloodshed. Woe to him who gives drink to his neighbors, pouring it till they are drunk. Woe to him who makes idols that cannot speak. But the Lord is in his holy temple; let all the earth be silent before him.
Habakkuk 2:6-20 (NIV)

i love **God** because

He turns my sorrow and sadness into joy.

. . . .

You turned my lament into dancing; You removed my sackcloth and clothed me with gladness, so that I can sing to You and not be silent. Lord my God, I will praise You forever. Psalm 30:11,12 (CSB)

i love **God** because

He is changing me to look like His son, Jesus.

. . . .

And we who with unveiled faces all reflect the Lord's glory, are being transformed into his likeness with ever-increasing glory.
2 Corinthians 3:18 (NIV)

i love **God** because

He can do anything He

wants. Nothing is too hard

for Him. Nothing!

. . . .

*I am the Lord, the God of all flesh. Is anything
too hard for me? Jeremiah 32:27 (ESV)*

i love God because

He uses "imperfect" people like Abraham

and David, Rahab and Ruth, and me to

accomplish His plans. Even the genealogy

of Jesus includes a lot of imperfect people.

. . . .

Abraham was the father of Isaac, …Salmon the father of Boaz by Rahab, and Boaz the father of Obed by Ruth, … and Jesse the father of David the king… and Jacob the father of Joseph the husband of Mary, of whom Jesus was born. Matthew 1:2-16 (ESV)

i love **God** because

He is extravagant in His love for me.

He is not stingy or half-hearted.

. . . .

How great is the love the Father has lavished on us, that we should be called children of God! And that is what we are!
1 John 3:1 (NIV)

i love
God because

He has great plans to bless me and

help me, not hurt me. He is purposeful

and intentional, not haphazard.

. . . .

For I know the plans I have for you, plans for good and not for evil,
to give you a future and a hope. Jeremiah 29:11 (NLT)

i love **God** because

little children were, and still are, important to Him.

. . . .

Take care lest you forget the things your eyes have seen, lest they depart from your heart. Make them known to your children and your children's children. Let the little children come to me. Deuteronomy 4:9; Matthew 19:14 (ESV)

i love **God** because

He made me in His image. We are not like the animals.

. . . .

God created man in his own image, in the image of God he created him; male and female he created them. God blessed them and said to them, "Be fruitful and increase in number; fill the earth and subdue it." Genesis 1:27,28 (NIV)

i love
God because

Jesus was willing to give

up **everything** to become a

servant to save **me.**

*Have this mind among yourselves, which is yours in Christ Jesus,
who, though he was in the form of God, did not count equality with
God a thing to be grasped, but made himself nothing, taking the
form of a servant…. he humbled himself by becoming obedient to
the point of death, even death on a cross.*
Philippians 2:5-8 (ESV)

i love
God because

He sent **Jesus** to show me the

way to eternal **life.** I don't

have to figure it out or

search **on my own.**

I am the way, the truth, and the life. No one comes to the Father except through me. John 14:6(ESV)

i love
God because

He will never forget about me.

He has engraved my name on

the palms of His hands!

. . . .

Can a mother forget the baby at her breast and have no compassion on the child she has borne? Though she may forget, I will not forget you! See, I have engraved you on the palms of my hands. Isaiah 49:15,16 (NIV)

i love
God because

He invented love and marriage,

home and family. Families

are important to Him.

. . . .

For this reason a man will leave his father and mother and be united to his wife, and the two will become one flesh. Ephesians 5:31 (NIV)

i love **God** because

He is sending Jesus back

to get me and take me home.

. . . .

We who are still alive at the Lord's coming will certainly have no advantage over those who have fallen asleep. For the Lord Himself will descend from heaven with a shout, with the archangel's voice, and with the trumpet of God, and the dead in Christ will rise first. Then we who are still alive will be caught up together with them in the clouds to meet the Lord in the air; and so we will always be with the Lord. Therefore encourage one another with these words.
1 Thessalonians 4:15-18 (CSB)